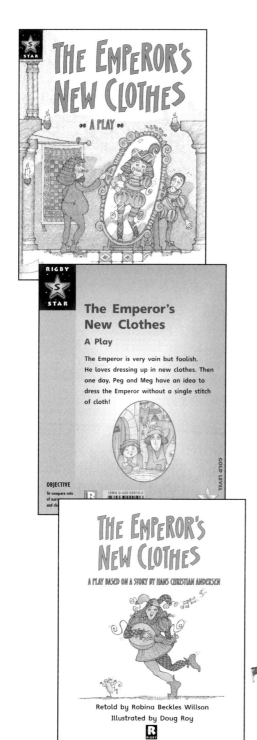

The front cover

What is happening in the picture? What is the Emperor wearing?

Why doesn't the Emperor see his real reflection in the mirror?

This is puzzling but the play will explain why.

The back cover

Let's read the blurb on the back cover.

Can you guess what Peg and Meg's idea is?

The title page

The person in the picture is a narrator. Does anyone know what a narrator is? (*a storyteller*)

What does the narrator do in a play? (*Tells the story from the side or front of the stage as it is happening.*)

Lesson 1

READ

Read pages 2 and 3

Purpose: To establish the characters in the play.

PAUSE

Pause at page 3

Ensure the children understand 'minister'. (*An important person who gives advice to the Emperor.*)

What do you think Peg and Meg do? How can you tell? (*scissors, pins, needle and thread*)

READ

Read pages 4 and 5 (Scene One)

Purpose: To find out what Peg and Meg think of the Emperor.

Talk the children through the layout of the first page, to establish that they understand it. Explain what 'Scene One' means. Explain that the narrator speaks in the past tense, while the characters speak in the present tense.

PAUSE

Pause at page 4

What do Peg and Meg think of the Emperor? Are they jealous of him? Why?

What do you think of Peg and Meg? Can you think of any words to describe them? (*lazy*) Which words or sentences tell you this? (E.g. *they did not want to do a lot of work*)

THE CHARACTERS

THE NARRATOR

THE EMPEROR

PEG AND MEG

A SMALL GIRL

THE MINISTER

2

3

SCENE ONE

In a town street, Peg and Meg are sitting doing nothing.

Narrator: Once upon a time, two women called Peg and Meg lived in a big town. They were always thinking of ways to make a lot of money. But they did not want to do a lot of work.

Peg: Our emperor is the richest man in this town.

Meg: He spends most of his money on clothes. He has different clothes for every day.

Peg: Every hour, more like it. I wish we could sell him some clothes. But we can't even weave.

Meg: That may not matter. I have an idea.

4

5

3

READ

Read pages 6 to 9 (Scene Two)

Purpose: To find out what Peg and Meg's plan is.

PAUSE

Pause at page 9

Where do Peg and Meg go?

Who do they meet first?

What big lie do they tell the Minister? (*We weave the best cloth in the world.*)

What does the Emperor ask to see? Do Peg and Meg have any cloth?

SCENE TWO

At the door of the emperor's palace. Two guards are standing by the entrance. Peg and Meg arrive. The minister opens the door.

Narrator: Peg and Meg arrive at the emperor's palace.

Peg: Good morning. We are Peg and Meg. We need to speak to the emperor's minister.

Minister: That's me. What can I do for you?

Meg: We want to speak to the emperor.

Minister: He is very busy at the moment, changing his clothes. Perhaps I can help. Come this way.

Peg and Meg go through the door into a large waiting room.

Peg: We need to speak to the emperor because we are weavers. We weave the best cloth in all the world.

Minister: I will ask the emperor if he has time to speak to you.

Peg: I hope he will come, Meg.

Emperor enters.

Meg: Look! Here he is!

Minister: These are the two weavers, Peg and Meg, Your Majesty.

Emperor: I can't see any cloth. What can you show me?

READ

Read pages 10 to 13

Purpose: To find out what is special about the cloth Peg and Meg say they can weave.

PAUSE

Pause at page 13

What is special about the cloth they say
they can weave? (*Check that children understand 'invisible'.*)

Do you think Peg and Meg can really do this?
Can they weave at all? Find evidence in the text to
support your view. (page 4 – *we can't even weave*)

Do you think the Emperor will believe them?
What does the Minister think? Does the Emperor agree?

Why do you think the Emperor will find this
suit useful?

Peg: If you give us the money to buy golden silk thread we can weave special cloth for you.

Meg: It will be very beautiful.

Peg: But it will also tell you who is foolish and who is very clever.

Minister: What cloth could do that?

Meg: Our cloth can do that because it is invisible to people who are foolish.

Emperor: You mean they just can't see it?

Peg: Yes, Your Majesty.

Emperor: Of course, I know that *I* am not foolish. In fact, I am very clever. But it might help me to know who is foolish. And who is *not* clever.

Meg: I'm sure it would be very useful, Your Majesty.

Peg: So, would you like us to weave you some of our special cloth?

Meg: And make you a new suit?

Emperor: Yes, at once. Minister, see that Peg and Meg have all they need.

READ

Read pages 14 and 15 (Scene Three)

Purpose: To find out what the Minister says when he visits Peg and Meg.

PAUSE

Pause at page 15

What does the Minister say? Is it the same as he's thinking?

Why does the Minister not say he couldn't see the cloth?

How do we know it's the Narrator talking on this page? (*written in past tense*)

Please turn to page 16 for Revisit and Respond activities.

SCENE THREE

Inside Peg and Meg's workshop. They are showing the minister how they weave the invisible cloth.

Narrator: The two women asked for a lot of silk and gold thread, as well as money. They set up their loom and began to weave. But they were only pretending. The loom was empty, and the thread was left in its bags.

Soon the emperor sent his minister to see how they were doing. The minister did not see any cloth, but he did not want to seem foolish, so he said nothing.

14

15

Lesson 2

RECAP

Recap lesson 1

What kind of book is this? (*a play*)

How is it different from a story?

Who are the characters, and what is the name of the person who tells the story?

What are Peg and Meg doing for the Emperor?

Why are they are doing this?

What is special about the cloth?

READ

Read pages 16 to 18 (Scene Four)

Purpose: To find out why Peg and Meg will work through the night.

PAUSE

Pause at page 18

Why did Meg say they would have to work through the night?

Will they really be working hard to get it finished? Why not?

What does Peg say to make the Emperor feel they are loyal citizens? (*We are glad to do that for Your Majesty.*)

Look at page 17. Which words almost give away the fact that the Emperor can't really see the cloth? (*Now, is THIS my cloth?*)

SCENE FOUR

Inside the palace throne room.

Minister: Peg and Meg are working hard, and the cloth is beautiful.

Emperor: I must see it for myself. Have it brought here at once.

Minister: Right away, Your Majesty. Everyone in the town has heard about this special cloth. They are longing to see it.

Minister leaves quickly.

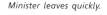

Minister enters with Peg and Meg.

Emperor: Now, is THIS my cloth?

Meg: Yes, Your Majesty. Isn't it beautiful?

Peg: I hope you like the colour.

Emperor: Yes, of course I do.

He is not sure.

Narrator: The emperor did not really see any cloth, but he did not want to seem foolish, so he said nothing.

Minister: You must have the suit ready for the procession tomorrow.

Meg: We will have to work all night!

Peg: But we are glad to do that for Your Majesty. I will cut out the suit at once.

READ

Read pages 19 to 21 (Scene Five)

Purpose: To find out how Meg and Peg persuade the Emperor that he is really wearing a suit.

PAUSE

Pause at page 21

What does Meg say to the Emperor to reassure him he is wearing the suit? (*This suit is so light,* etc.)

What does the Emperor say which makes us think he's not sure he's wearing the suit for the parade? (*it's cold today*)

Why do you think the Minister joins in with persuading the Emperor?

SCENE FIVE

At the workshop of Peg and Meg.

Narrator: The next day, the emperor and his minister went to see the weavers.

Peg: This suit is so light, it will seem as if you are wearing almost nothing. Would you like to try it on over by the big mirror?

19

Meg: Then we can help you put on your new suit.

Peg: And this beautiful new cloak. You will need two people to walk behind you, carrying it.

Meg: Do the trousers fit, Your Majesty?

Peg: And the jacket?

Emperor: Yes, yes. But it is a cold day to go walking in a procession.

Minister: A lot of people are waiting to see you.

Emperor: Of course, they always like seeing my new clothes.

20

21

READ

Read pages 22 to the end (Scene Six)

Purpose: To find out who tells the truth about the suit.

PAUSE

Pause at page 24

Who was brave enough to tell the truth? Why did nobody else tell the truth?

Why did Peg and Meg and the Minister say 'Shhh!' to the little girl?

What did the Emperor do when he realized he was in his underwear?

Which words tell us how he was feeling? (*cold/foolish*)

Can you think of any other words to describe how the Emperor might be feeling?

Who were the foolish characters in the end?

SCENE SIX

The procession through town. The emperor is walking along wearing only his underwear.

Narrator: The emperor was at the head of the procession. Everyone said that his new clothes were beautiful. Nobody wanted to say they could not see his clothes. They did not want to seem foolish, or not clever. But . . .

Girl: Look, Mum! The emperor is in his underwear!

Peg, Meg and Minister: Ssh!

Girl: But, Mum, he's only wearing his underwear!

Peg, Meg and Minister: Ssh!

Girl: Why is the emperor only wearing his underwear, Mum?

Peg, Meg and Minister: Ssh!

22

23

Narrator: The emperor heard the girl, and then he heard everyone quietly agree that he only had his underwear on. All he could do was keep walking, with his head held high. He felt very cold and very foolish.

24

After Reading

Revisit and Respond

Lesson 1

(T) Who do you think are the cleverest characters in the play, and why?

(T) Look at page 4 with the children. Ask them to change Peg and Meg's speech into the past tense as though the Narrator is speaking. Discuss any other differences between the characters' speech and the Narrator's.

(T) What do you think will happen when the Emperor tries on his clothes? Why won't he want to tell the truth?

(T) Sort the children into five parts – Narrator, Peg, Meg, Minister, Emperor, and read the play so far.

Lesson 2

(T) Re-enact the play, with children taking the characters' parts. Emphasize reading with expression.

(T) Who begins and ends the play? (*Narrator*) What is the Narrator's job?

(T) Role-play a conversation between Peg and Meg at the end of the story.

(S) Write question words (*what, how, why, when, who, where*) on cards. Ask a child to volunteer as a 'hot seat' character and to take the role of the minister. Other children ask the minister questions, prompted by the question cards. (E.g. *What do you think the people at the procession will say? Why didn't you tell the truth?*)

(W) Brainstorm words to describe the emperor, Peg and Meg.